I0107871

THE BROKEN TUSK

Seeing Through the Lens of Vedanta

by Daniel McKenzie

Broken Tusk Press

Copyright © 2018 Daniel McKenzie

All rights reserved

This paperback edition presents the essays in a more spacious form, closer to how they were originally contemplated. The order in which the essays are presented has also changed.

ISBN: 979-8-9897339-7-2

www.thebrokentusk.com

Contents

Introduction

This is not a book about Vedanta—a venerable wisdom tradition that has enlightened thousands of people over centuries based on empirical and impeccable logic—it's a book seen through Vedanta. What follows is not scriptural commentary or philosophical argument, but the trace of what remains when those teachings settle into the heart and begin to reshape how one sees the world.

Vedanta describes three phases of Self-inquiry. The first stage involves listening. Just listening can be a difficult task for most. We all have beliefs about who we are, about the world, and perhaps, even about God that we've carried with us since childhood—not to mention a certain reluctance to admit that some of those beliefs might be wrong. Vedanta asks inquirers at this stage to sit down, shut up, and ask questions later. Needless to say, it requires an open mind because much of what Vedanta teaches is counterintuitive to how we've been brought up to see things.

During the second stage the inquirer contemplates what they have heard and asks questions to clarify what, up until now, might have only been accepted based on faith. Inquirers are encouraged to eliminate every doubt until they see the truth in what Vedanta teaches. Vedanta can be challenging, not because of its seemingly encrypted content, but because ignorance is hard-wired.

The last stage may be the concluding stage of one's spiritual development, but it isn't final. There is no *Enlightenment Certificate of Achievement* once you have a little knowledge under your belt, because the last leg of our journey is the on-going assimilation and application of the knowledge. And it is from this stage that these writings come from.

These essays are the outcome of absorbing the teachings and observing experience through a different lens. They are a journal of reflection and contemplation. This is where the "rubber meets the road," as they say, because knowledge can only really be made useful once applied and tested. Only then, through the grittiness of life, can we arrive a little closer to the freedom Vedanta shows us.

Daniel McKenzie
September 2018

Vedanta

Life appears to be an impossible equation
until you find the answer.

And if you are diligent enough,
once you find the answer,
you will try to disprove it.

You will try to find holes in—
places where the numbers don't add up.

Vedanta is the limit.
It's as far as the inner eye can see.
It's the end of seeking
—not due to some naive acceptance,
but because nothing else works.

Vedanta is like a math equation
that no matter how many times you do it,
it always comes out right.

When our mind becomes dull,
we need an equation we can rely on
something that reminds us
that through the application of knowledge,
there lies the truth.
Vedanta is that math equation

that I continue to use
even after I know the answer.

It's that equation I return to
over
and over again
to show me that I'm seeing things as they are,
and not just as they appear to be.

Rattle Rattle Rattle

The mind is like
a home appliance
that rattles
when it's running.

Waking up in the morning,
we are a witness
to all kinds of thoughts
from the day before:

likes,
dislikes,
regrets—
things seen,
spoken,
read and heard.

Should we get upset
if the machinery
rattles a bit?

Nothing in this world
operates
without making
a little noise.

By the Power of My Maya

As Einstein—or someone—once put it:

"We can will ourselves to act,
but we cannot will ourselves
to will."

So what is it
that's willing us
to will?

Would the man
behind the curtain
please step out.

See the trick?

This is the power of *maya*,
the macrocosmic
causal body
at work.

Where's the doer?

This Ignorance

Our biggest challenge was never
putting a man on the moon,
it has always been
stepping out of our ignorance.

They say the truth is eternal,
and as old as the hills—
and yet, here we are,
still suffering the same ailments.

Paradise isn't heaven.
Paradise is man,
minus his ignorance.

Shall we ever get to paradise?

Maybe we're just a society of rebels
who needs to have its fill and poison
before realizing the truth.

Maybe we'll eventually tire of
consumerism,
politics,
religion
adventure-seeking—
just enough to turn within.

But probably not.

A few individuals will see
that there's no winning here,
that the world is built
to frustrate us
into finding moksha.

Seen through this lens,
our ignorance is both
our master
and our liberator.

In other words,
ignorance has a role.
It has significance.

For those lucky enough
to discover the truth,
ignorance is a means to an end.

As for the rest?

Life may be nothing more
than a series
of ongoing disappointments.

Dumb and Dumber

Why is it
that we only use the word
"ignorant"
to describe man
but not nature?

We don't talk about
ignorant forests
or complain about
naive oceans.

There are no
halfwitted dragon flies
or unschooled ants,
no doltish rocks,
moronic volcanoes, or
imbecilic protoplasm.

Why is man
the only
self-proclaimed
dumb-ass
here?

Judging Others

Often when I travel
and have time
to people-watch,
I become judgmental.

And then
I become judgmental
of my judging.

I wonder:
if everyone were just like me,
would I still be judgmental?

Of course!

I would see all my faults
and wonder
why I couldn't be
a more perfect version
of "me."

I would get impatient with others
for being quiet and unsocial—
and later,
for being restless and silly.

I would criticize them
for eating the wrong foods,
for not standing up
to their teenagers,
for not taking care
of their front yards,
for driving too fast,
for spending too much time
on the computer,
and for picking their nose
in public
when they thought
no one was looking.

Most of all,
I would be skeptical
of what they were thinking
and how they were constantly
judging me!

Funny thing is,
it is all me.

It's all just me
buried under countless bodies,
histories,
tendencies,
likes and dislikes,
and thoughts—
lots of thoughts.

Some days,
it's hard
to get my head
wrapped around this
and stop judging
"the others."

There really is
just one operating system here.

The truth is,
we're all just sharing
the one Self—
and it's all me.

It's Not Personal

Perhaps it's easier
if you're a visual artist—
in particular, someone
who studied artistic anatomy.

If so, you're most likely familiar
with anatomical variations in people:
like the unusual folds some ears have,
the awkward large head of a young child,
or the way a nose-job
can distort the natural balance of the face.

And if the nuances of others interest you,
you are probably equally—
if not more—
interested in the variations
of your own physical appearance.

After all,
aren't we constantly looking in the mirror
to see what else we can find?
To find out what has changed
since the last time we looked?

You've probably at one time said something like,
"I have my mother's eyes,"

or "I have my father's hands."

We all take pride—
or feel disappointment—
in inheriting certain traits
from our parents.

But it's much more than that.

If you look closely,
you'll notice that you're really
just pieces of Mom and Dad
from head to toe.

Mostly Mom and Dad parts
stitched together,
with perhaps a few others
that snuck in
from mutations in your DNA.

After appreciating that your body
is just an inherited, ancestral
genetic quilt,
you might next come
to the realization
that nowhere is there "me"—

not your nose,
not your eyes,
not your mouth,

not even that pimple
on your bum.

In fact, what you think of as "me"
is mostly just
a different arrangement
of what came before.

"You" are a composite.

But such is the universe—
recycled parts.

And if you can't hold claim
to any inch of your body,
then what of your mind?

I'm not saying your mind
 is Mom and Dad.
We've all been shaped
by our environment
in different and unique ways.

But there are probably
similar tendencies in there.
Wouldn't you agree?

Which just goes to show:
the deeper you dig,
the more impersonal it gets— and the harder it
becomes to find "me."

Variations

We all wonder
how our lives would have been
had we done it differently.

Truth is,
it couldn't have been
any different.

What makes you think
you would've made
different choices
given the same circumstances?

"You" are not even
making the choices.

God knows exactly
what will happen to you
tomorrow
and the next day,
and the next.

Because when you're able
to factor in
all the different constants
and variables

(which only God can do),
cause and effect is like a math equation
with only one outcome.

Still,
we can't help
but wonder
about all the possibilities.

Maya, the Original Time Machine

Everyone imagines
how they will be
when they are
60,
80,
even 100 years old.

We imagine
getting old
will happen
many,
many
years
from now.

However, once we get there
we will marvel
at how quickly
time has passed—

and what seemed like
"many, many years from now"
will feel like
only
a few minutes ago.

Of course,
the real marvel
isn't the passing of time
but the illusion
of it actually passing.

For that,
we can thank *maya*.
Maya is the original
time machine.

Treadmill

Samsara really comes down
to running in place.

We think we're moving,
making progress,
but really,
it's only the illusion
of time and space
moving against
the static screen
of awareness.

Legs are a-danglin',
arms are a-flappin',
but we're not actually
going anywhere.

Against the backdrop
of awareness,
there is no progress.

There is no forward,
backward,
up,
or down.

The whole world
is just an elaborate stage
designed
to encourage
more running.

Why do you think
they call it
a treadmill?

A Trip to Costco

February 11, 2018

If you have never been to Costco, it can be like going to another planet. I had been to the mega warehouse shopping club before, but it had been a while (maybe two years?) and had forgotten how it felt. I was originally just supposed to wait for my wife in the car while she picked up a few things, but as soon as we parked I felt like exploring and decided to go in.

The first thing I noticed as we approached the entrance were the giant shopping carts. They look like something Fred Flintstone would use to pick up a few of his super-size dinosaur ribs. The extra-wide shopping carts should really be the brand symbol of Costco (and of our consumer society). Just looking at them gave me a chuckle.

I was surprised nobody else was doing the same as little women half the cart's size, pushed them around with their bounty inside: 48-roll packages of toilet paper, "4-pak" loaves of bread, cake-size boxes of frozen chicken wings, a couple of dog mattresses for Fido, and a grease-laden cardboard box with a cold pizza inside for the family at home.

Costco has the same vibe of an amusement park. There, you can observe all kinds of people, each hankering to fulfill his or her desires in a feast for the senses. Costco advertises the benefit of warehouse prices, but I believe the real reason people like to shop there is because it's okay to want multiples of everything—chocolate cakes, HD plasma screens, socks, underwear…whatever your fancy.

Bottom line: Nobody at Costco is going to judge you for being an absolute glutton.

People wheel down the aisles with their Fred Flintstone shopping carts grabbing and trying samples of food at every aisle cap. They are all running the same algorithm, unconscious of the forces that compel them to forage and stock up while it's available in front of them. This is what gives them their obvious zombie appearance—and maybe they are real zombies for all I know.

I couldn't help but get a very "nobody's home" feeling. I'm sure had I stopped to talk with any of them that wouldn't have been the case, but from the outside it appeared that these weren't actual people, but rather, humanoids running on high-octane *rajoguna*.

Even the employees in their hair nets serving samples appeared to be nothing more than rudimentary android models built for the single task of handing out enticing treats to the ravenous zombies. Don't get me wrong: they were pleasant and all, and fulfilled their task beautifully. But only half there, really.

Their robotic movements and the responses of the zombies put me in a sort of hypnotic state, as if I was an actual visitor from another planet quietly observing the extraterrestrial life before me.

Looking back, my experience at Costco was most interesting due to my understanding of what was happening. In Vedanta's terms, I was in *samsara*. I was witnessing the impersonal and unconscious forces that drive all human beings. At the same time, I was also witnessing how my own program was responding to *maya's* tricks.

When we first arrived at Costco my perception of its binding nature was as clear as day—even to the point of laughing out loud at the absurdity of it all. But by the time we had spent a good thirty-minutes there, I was beginning to find the objects interesting and feeling more comfortable with the exotic landscape.

The scene was normalizing for me and the original shock of being transported to a different planet was wearing off.

Sometimes I find it hard to believe that we humans all come from the same mold. Why isn't everyone clamoring for enlightenment begging to escape this *samsara*? True, I am the Self and so are you.

It's a bit creepy to think that you and I are the same, that it's all just me, and that all beings, including this one, exist in me. It's even stranger to think that the person I believe I am is just a robot and so are you.

However, it's reassuring to know I am the Self. Because as humans, we are just too (wait for it) alien.

Use by Expiration Date

All objects
have an expiration date.

Not in the long-term certainty
that eventually they will be discarded,
Crumble,
and disintegrate—

but in the other unavoidable truth
that they will someday
stop providing us pleasure.

Sometimes this reality
becomes a frustration,
like when the music
you used to love
no longer does it for you—
when even silence
is preferable
to listening to any one
of the 10,000 songs
you bought on iTunes.

Thus,
our never-ending search
for more-better-different.

Vedanta is right
when it says
not to hang your hat
on object-oriented happiness.

This kind of happiness,
by nature,
is uncertain,
Fleeting,
and unreliable.

And we're not just talking
about the kind of happiness
that requires a lot of maintenance
and upkeep—
like owning a boat
or sustaining
a passionate romantic relationship—

we're talking about
actual expiration dates,
like the kind you see
on a carton of milk
or a loaf of bread.

Let's face it:
eventually that $3,000
mid-century black walnut
coffee table you bought last month
is going to blend in

with all your other knick-knacks
and cease to provide you
with much,
if any,
pleasure.

This is a fact,
not a likelihood.

This is *samsara*.
And it's why they say
life is a setup.

If this weren't the case,
you would still be playing
with all your childhood toys—
because they would still be providing you
with hours of enjoyment.

Where are your
G.I. Joe,
Micronauts,
Atari 2600 game console, or
Pet Rock now?

What about your first car?

Remember when going to the arcade
or playing mini-golf
was still fun?

Why do you still clean out
your wardrobe each year,
change diets,
switch gyms,
and seek out
new vacation spots?

So, if life is a setup,
what is it setting us up for?

What's the message?

Should we just continue
to seek out
one temporary—
and ultimately, unsatisfactory—
joy after another?

What happens when old age,
financial restraints,
war,
or a natural disaster
restrict our ability
to tap into certain joys?

But what if
there's another way?

What is it
that never expires

and is a permanent source
of happiness?

What if it's closer
than you think?

What if it's closer to you
than, let's say,
your nose?

Nobody Wants Your Stuff

Nobody will want your stuff
after you're gone.

No one will want your artwork,
your furniture,
your tools or any of the things
that you kept so close.

They won't want it!

They won't want
your pricey perfume,
your clothes,
your shoes,
or your Louis Vuitton.

They won't want
your jewelry,
your watches,
and they'll have no idea
what to do
with your wedding band.

They won't want your Christmas ornaments—
or any ornaments
for any holiday

or any season.

They won't want it!

They won't want your book collection,
stamp collection,
CD collection, DVD collection—
or any collection.

And they'll have no idea
what to do
with all those letters
you kept for years.

They won't want it!

Nobody will want your stuff.

Why?

Because your stuff
only pleases you.

Which just goes to show:
joy is not in the object,
and it's certainly
not in your stuff.

They won't want it!

Why Would You?

"Oh, how funny.

You mean,
you… you actually thought
all those objects,
people,
and experiences
were there
for you to have?

You mean,
you never caught on—
never thought,
even once,
that it might all be
a setup?

Why would you think…?

I mean,
when you die
you have to leave
everything!

Wait—
why would you think…

that…
this…

Oh,
never mind."

A Little Spiritual Exercise

Men,
here's a little spiritual exercise
to help remind yourself
you are not the body:

Yank out
one of those ugly,
twisted,
thick,
cable-like
nose "hairs"
growing like
an invasive plant species
from inside
your nostrils.

Take a good look at it—
a really good look.

Now ask yourself:

Is this
me?

Samsari

"More,
more,
more.

Better,
better,
better.

Different,
different,
different.

Pleeeeeaaaaase—
something
just to make me feel
adequate,
whole
and complete!

Sometimes I feel like
I'm not even doing this.

My desires?
Yes,
they must be indulged.

If not, there are consequences—
like that annoying,
gnawing,
empty feeling.

Plus,
everyone else
is doing it!

All my co-workers,
friends and family.

I have to keep up!

This is just
the way life is.

We work our asses off so we can have nice things
and AMAZING EXPERIENCES!!!

Got a problem with that?"

- *Samsari*

Impersonal Forces

The disturbing daily events
and history of man
are nothing but a constant
course correction
in relationship to the physical,
Psychological,
and moral laws of the universe—
better known as the dharma field.

Forces bump into
the wall of the field,
which in turn cause
opposing forces
to be pushed back
within their set boundaries.

The inevitable result
is a restoration
of balance
and harmony.

In spite of all appearances,
the drama of life
and world events
is nothing but God
bouncing off

the restraining walls
of its own creation.

A few men and women
may live to brag
about scaling the wall,
but they don't do so
for very long.

When they finally come down,
it's usually
with a loud splat!

Viewed from this perspective,
the drama of life
loses its threatening appearance,
and dispassion
naturally arises.

It also gives meaning
to the fact that the world
is perfect the way it is
and cannot be otherwise.

After all,
from Vedanta's point of view,
the world's apparent chaos
is just impersonal forces
ricocheting off
the aforementioned walls.

Those who take the chaotic world
to be a battle
between "good"
and "evil"
miss the point.

There is no good and evil—
just the conditions
of unconscious
internal
and external forces
making their course corrections.

Sometimes these forces
ricochet
like tennis balls being
thrown in a small room.

But all forces
eventually wind down,
as they must,
until stirred again.

What are these impersonal forces?

The gunas[1].

[1] The three basic constituents of creation (intelligence, energy, matter) as used by God to create, sustain and dissolve the world. Within the mind, the gunas also act as impersonal mental conditions that must be managed by the individual in order to lead a peaceful life.

Power

All of us have certain degrees of power—
power that influences others.

It's not magic,
but it might as well be.

When we're young, we often admire the powers of
others and try to emulate it—mostly to our disappointment (because you cannot pretend power). In
youth, we want the power of physical attractiveness,
charisma, and that of popular athletes, musicians and
celebrities. As we get older, we want the more refined
power of successful business leaders, politicians,
poets and gurus.

Some of us discover our own power early in life,
while others much later. Some of us, blind to their
use or importance, never realize their power or
perhaps never learn of its existence. There are different degrees of power. For example, we might be
creative and exhibit sparks of genius early in life, but
not have enough will to sustain it, to hold onto it, to
cultivate it.

All powers in the end, have one goal:
to influence the world;

to have some control.

Powers are magical in that they allow an individual to do things others cannot. Where doors open for one, they won't open for others—no matter how much you try.

No matter how much you try, you could never play basketball like LeBron James. No matter how much you try, you could never make a company like Elon Musk. No matter how much you try, you could never act a part like Meryl Streep.

Powers not only influence, they enchant, charm, even put one under a spell. The spell might be evoked by a smile, tone of voice, or gesture. When I catch myself in the moment admiring someone, I observe their power. What is it? What did he or she just do to captivate me and their audience? What was the technique? Is it one power or a mixture of powers? Is it real power or just the illusion of confidence that most people feign when they don't know what they're doing (which occurs most of the time).

How about powers for good?
The power of kindness, compassion, acceptance?

We mustn't always view power cynically. After all, these powers don't belong to anyone in particular, they are God-given. They are God's way of keeping the creation moving.

When I observe people, I no longer just see them as people, but as power-wielding *jivas*. The world is all of a sudden more interesting and less mundane when you realize all the magic around us: the dancer with perfect movement, the guru that shows the logic, the politician that cuts through the cynicism, the CEO that inspires innovation.

But what greater power than the power to know who you are?

All the world's great politicians, artists and intellects are just actors on God's stage. But how many of them actually know that?

What greater power is there than the power of Self-knowledge?

Self-knowledge is the power that surpasses all powers. It's the power that sees other powers for what they really are, just temporary, impersonal feats of fancy.

Science

The problem with science
is that it's limited
to what we can perceive
with the senses
and infer
with the intellect.

Scientists assume
that consciousness
arose out of inert matter,

But how can that be?

The more logical conclusion
turns everything around
by stating that
the world isn't out there—
the world is in you.

In other words,
objects rise
out of consciousness.

That means consciousness
is the substrate
and everything else

is just superimposed.

The mind is like
a virtual reality player
and I
am just the witness.

Thus, non-duality is a much more elegant answer
than thinking
we can squeeze consciousness
out of dead matter.

Will scientists ever find
the cause of consciousness?

No—
because they're looking
in the wrong direction.

Zoomed In, Zoomed Out

The truth that Vedanta teaches
makes more sense when juxtaposed with how the
individual
experiences life on a daily basis.

Zoomed-in, life on the surface
is never what it seems.

It's only when we're able to zoom out
and look at things
from a 40,000 foot view
that we are able see the truth.

Here are some examples.

Free Will

Zoomed-in:
Because I have an intellect, I have free will.
I am able to make choices
and fulfill actions based on those choices.
I don't have control of everything,
but I pretty much do what I want
whenever circumstances are in my favor.

Zoomed-out:
There is no free will.
You are controlled by universal laws,
your conditioned likes and dislikes,
and impersonal forces
that have the power
to alternately conceal, project and reveal.

As a result,
the world for you (and everyone else)
is constantly changing.

God calls all the shots.
Personal control is an illusion.

Self

Zoomed-in:
I am myself—an individual.
I have a body, a name, a history,
and set of preferences.
I also have a mind
along with all my thoughts and emotions.

Zoomed-out:
There is only the impersonal Self,
the one without a second.

Through a process of negation

it becomes clear
that you are not the body-mind.
You are the smallest derivative—
pure awareness.

The ego is just an illusion,
a by-product caused by *maya*
and the Self's proximity
to the body-mind.

World

Zoomed-in:
All physical objects are real
because they feel real.
If they weren't real I could, for example,
walk in front of a moving car
and not get hurt.

If my senses tell me something is real,
it's real.
I kick a rock
and stub my toe.
It's real.

Zoomed-out:
The world is not real—
it's only apparently real.

The world cannot be validated,
as we never actually come into contact
with objects;
all objects only exist as thoughts.

Furthermore, the world is ephemeral,
with objects constantly changing,
coming and going.

All objects, when investigated,
are made of other parts
and don't stand on their own.

Scripture says
objects exist in me,
but I am not the objects.

Only the Self is real.

God

Zoomed-in:
God is creator, sustainer
and dissolver of the universe.
God watches over all
and makes judgment.
I must negotiate with God
if I want to lead a happy life.

Zoomed-out:
God is a mysterious power
that creates the appearance of objects.

The essence of God is awareness,
which is your essence and everyone else's essence too.

God and God's creation
are only apparently real.

God exists in me, the Self,
but I am not God.

Everything resolves into awareness—
even God.

History

September 14, 2018

After watching Ken Burns' PBS video series about the West, I came to the conclusion that as interesting as U.S. history is with all its different characters and story lines, it and all history can be summed up as the unsuccessful pursuit of object-oriented happiness.

Over and over again, throughout history, we see man inflict suffering upon himself and others due to desire for objects. We see man inflict suffering on their spouses, their family, friends, community and country.

In the history of the West, it's apparent in the frontiersmen who put their families in extreme danger for want of their own land, in the Mormon founders' revision of Christianity in exchange for absolute power, in the railroad tycoons using (and later, throwing out) the Chinese like disposable widgets, in the lies and killings directed toward the extinction of Native Americans, and of course, in the 49'ers who stopped at nothing to extract riches from the earth.

And don't think it was just the Neo-Americans.

Previous Spanish inhabitants were equally lustful in their own search for riches and their desire to convert a native population to Catholicism (a clever psychological means to control the indigenous population in a way that was both cost efficient and didn't require armies of men to keep them down). Nor were the Native American Indians, saints. There were plenty of over-zealous warriors from tribes willing to capture, imprison, enslave, kill and push their neighbors out for territorial gain.

…And on and on it goes,
where it stops nobody knows.

Man's pursuit of object-oriented happiness is beginningless and continues unabated today at breakneck speed thanks to the internet and other recent technologies. This is man's insanity. It's man's fever, regardless of race, nationality, location or time.

Doesn't man see that all his greed leads nowhere? Doesn't man see that it's all just a "chasing after the wind"? That once your basic needs are met the rest is just vanity? Doesn't man see that a hundred years from now hardly anyone will remember their name or have a care about all the wealth and power they once amassed?

I could go on and on describing how illogical and absurd it is and how it's a psychosis. It's inexplainable, that is, until we learn of the source. Greed is just a symptom of Self-ignorance, of not knowing who we are. Greed is the impossible mission of trying to satisfy our inner ghost, a non-existent entity—the ego—which is nothing more than a strange byproduct of the intellect reinforced by beliefs, family and society at large.

Buddhism with its Four Noble Truths teaches that desire in the form of grasping causes suffering. Whatever we hold too tightly eventually comes back to hold us in negative ways. Unfortunately, the Buddha forgot to mention another truth—that the cause of our desire is our mistaken identity.

Our whole bloody history is about a mistaken identity, and you can count on it that our future will be more of the same.

Man is the soul under a spell. Nobody chooses to be driven by greed. Nobody chooses to be ignorant and to suffer as a result. Who would make such a choice? Who would pursue something they know in the end would bring suffering to themselves and those around them? Who would pursue a path to self-destruction?

In the end, nobody is doing anything. Nobody is doing the impersonal forces that drive us, nor is anyone doing their conditioning.

From a macrocosmic view, history looks like God playing.

This is God's amazing story or game—and the game doesn't work unless there's *maya*: a mysterious power that exists within awareness and makes the impossible, possible. According to Vedanta, *maya* is not only responsible for every physical object in creation, but for every thought, desire and fear.

The ultimate maze in this game is that which leads the individual to find out that the master/creator of the game is also the player; that God is the game, the game pieces, and the game rules. It's God's game that it plays with itself.

Why does God need a means to know itself?
Why the game?
Why why why?

Nobody knows the reason—not even the sages.

Our only salvation is knowing maya or ignorance isn't real; that it ceases to exist provided the right knowledge. This is all just God's dreamscape projecting on the screen of awareness.

It's God's most amazing experience.

The show is playing.

The actors are performing.
And we are its captive audience.

The Truth Hidden in Plain Sight

It almost seems trivial
that people complain
day in and day out
about all the injustices
in the world.

It's as if we had
a skin disease
and instead of trying
to find its cause,
we complained all day
about the rash.

We talk about
its redness,
its itchiness,
its size
and depth.

Its ability
to make us irritable,
cause depression,
make us miss work,
and keep us away
from what we love to do.

We talk about
how many people have it
and in which regions
of the world.

We talk about
its history—
past,
present,
and future.

We write books about it.
We build museums.
We create websites
to educate others.

We do everything
except
find a cure.

People have much invested
in their beliefs.

They're a source of comfort,
I suppose.

Unfortunately,
most people would rather
be right
than be happy.

It's the ego again—
always getting in the way.

The world is insane,
driven mad
by the powers of *maya*.

We go round and round
on the *maya*-go-round
of *samsara*,
never able
to get off.

We're stuck
because we can't see past
our conditioning—
the likes and dislikes
that keep us spinning
in a centrifuge
of suffering.

Politics and the media
are just the chattering
of an unwitting society

the masses floundering
in the dark
a lot of complaining
about a rash
that will never go away,

no matter how loudly
we protest.

So what is a yogi
to do?

The wise step lightly
and carefully—
as if walking
on a geese-infested
golf course.

They see everyone
as puppets,
hypnotized
by *maya's* powers.

They see them
as children
in adult body-suits,
carrying adult responsibilities.

But mostly,
they see the Self—
"me"—
and the truth
that remains hidden
from them.

A Zero-Sum Game

Unlike some other traditions,
a teacher of Vedanta won't just tell you
that you're the Self
and then ask you
to discuss it amongst yourselves.

They usually begin
with something a bit easier to chew on.

For example,
they might start off stating the obvious:
that life is a zero-sum game—
for every up
there's a down.

It's easy to recognize this
when you look at celebrities
and politicians
who think they have everything
—until they don't.

But I always wondered
how the zero-sum teaching applies
to a starving child in Africa.

I can see how a rich

and famous person's life
would be equalized
by the zero-sum game,
but not one that is starving
and weakened by extreme poverty.

Where's the upside
to starving to death?

I suppose the silver lining
for a starving and dying child
is that suffering
doesn't just go on forever.

In extreme cases,
the finality of death
serves as a welcome refuge—
a merciful "up"
where there was no one before.

Death is probably the only situation
where it's hard to imagine
a hidden upside.

But I believe the teaching
still holds water
in every situation.

Similar to death,
even war has its hidden upsides.

For example,
destruction is always followed
by rebirth.

Paradoxically,
the ugliness of war
can only be seen
against the backdrop of peace.

Samsara is a world
where opposites come and go
like the weather.

Opposites are part
of the natural order of things.
They are how the field operates.

Another point is this:

Taken at a macrocosmic level,
the death of a child—
or many children—
may bring attention to the problem
and ultimately safeguard
thousands more
from suffering the same fate.

In this case,
a relatively smaller percentage
may need to die

for the survival of the greater.

God always does
what's in the best interest
of the Total.

God is always trying
to strike a balance.

From this perspective,
God is like an intelligent machine—
taking everything into account
and conducting on-going system checks.

The zero-sum teaching
is really a lesson
about God's universal laws
(call it nature, if you prefer).

Life is a zero-sum game because,
if it weren't,
only the extremes would ensue,
birthing greater extremes,
and not before long, the world would fall apart.

Extremes in the field of experience
don't just go on infinitely.

There are no winners here,
nor are there losers.

There is only
the balance of forces—
call it dharma.

As usual,
it's only our ignorance of the truth
that creates suffering
in response to these changing conditions.

Ultimately,
we are what's beyond
life's ups and downs.

Only in that realization
do we find
actual freedom.

Lila

"The reward is the drama."
— *The Tick*

If the universe was built
so that God could play
(the lila theory),
then why all the pain,
sorrow
and suffering?

The Self isn't here to play—
the Self has no desires
or attributes.

And if God created the universe
for play,
why did he make
our happiness
so temporary?

Why not make it easy
and provide
infinite pleasure
for everyone?

Maybe God created the world

for the drama.

Like a good movie,
God sits back
and watches
all the conflict
and resolution
and is intrigued by it.

After all,
there's not much interest
in having everyone
just be happy
all the time.

A movie without both
a protagonist
and an antagonist
doesn't make
for a very compelling story.

Where's the glory
without a struggle?

What's a hero
without a conflict?

People think
all their pain
and suffering

is real.

Little do they know
they're just movie characters
playing out their parts
in a dream
being dreamt by God.

But this brings us
to the question:

Why would God need
to be entertained
in the first place?

God isn't a person
who gets bored
and begins to fidget.

God doesn't have preferences—
only laws.

It all goes back
to the mysterious power
of *maya*,
for which
there is no answer.

Oh, well.

Sin

I often have the frustrating feeling
that everything is wrong about the world.

I've always known it,
but only now can understand this feeling—
that most everything
is off the mark.

This feeling is really about sensing
what's true
and what isn't.

It's also why,
when I'm in nature,
I don't have the feeling.

The world constructed by man
makes us uneasy
because it goes against
our true nature.

When man knows who he is,
he's in balance.
He's following dharma.
He can take it easy,
knowing that everything is okay.

When man doesn't know who he is,
which is most of the time,
he is off the mark,
which is
the original definition
of
"sin."

You see,
man doesn't know
he's the Self
and instead believes
he's the body-mind.

His environment reflects this error
in every way.

And as a result,
those who are able
to discern the truth intuitively,
feel that something is wrong—
that what's lacking
is a fundamental truth.

And they're right.

Our Duty

Let's face it—
life is overrated.

I know it's taboo to say that,
but deep inside
everyone knows it
and is just afraid
to state the obvious.

Why?

Because by saying it,
we're afraid
we might let the air
out of the balloon—
the will
to continue.

If life were so great,
we'd spend more time
expressing it.

All art would be
an expression
of our love for life.

History would be
a celebration—
not a record
of conflict.

But the fact is,
life is tough.

We sense
the preciousness of life.
We sense
the richness of love
when it's offered.

And yet,
we constantly struggle
to keep our chins up
in the face
of all the perceived negatives.

True—
love and bliss
are available
here and now.

But only under
almost impossible conditions—
conditions
that are hard
to maintain,

and even harder
to make constant.

There is no enlightenment.
Only the ongoing recognition
that, due to certain
personal imperfections,
I'm unable
to remain happy.

It makes me want to protest:

Thank you,
old wise sage,
for clarifying things—
but I'm kind of
psychologically stuck
in this dream-waking thing
and can't seem
to just pretend
that I'm not real
and the world isn't either!

But maybe
that's all part
of the master plan.

We're not here
to find the next
best experience.

We're here
to do the work.

And the pain
we experience every day—
great or small—
is a reminder of that.

It's as if Krishna
on the battlefield
were saying to Arjuna:

Get off your ass
and do your job!

All those things
you take pleasure in?
All those hopes,
attachments,
and grievances?

They're all traps—
traps meant
to break you
and put you
on the pathless path!
Get in line, soldier!

DO
YOUR
DUTY!

Until we see
our true duty,
until we see ourselves
as slayers of ignorance
on the field of experience,
it's just
one damn thing
after another.

Life is frustrating
because we don't understand
our duty—
our dharma.

It's all dharma.

Live it—
or suffer.

Fear

Most people are sadly unaware
of the most basic causes of their suffering.

It's as if they walk through life
with a pebble in their shoe.

They complain and cry out loud
to everyone about their suffering
without ever taking notice
of the reasons why.

For those blessed
with some Self-knowledge,
it's hard not to feel
like the smartest kid in the class.

One begins to wonder
if most of the population
isn't severely retarded
in their spiritual development.

You want to shake them and say,

"Hey, you've got a huge fucking rock
in your shoe
and ALL YOU NEED TO DO

IS TAKE IT OUT!"

I suppose Vedanta's explanation
is that we're in a sort of karma matrix
until we gain enlightenment.

But even then,
we still have our leftover karma
to deal with.

In other words,
you're stuck in this kindergarten
until you finally figure it out—
and even then,
you must still find a way
to deal with all the snot-nosed kids.

The conundrum
is that the snot-nosed kids
aren't so stupid.

Some of them are actually
quite smart.

In fact,
many of them are smarter than you.

The problem
is they can't see.
A blind man may have

great intelligence,
but no amount of smarts
is going to make him see color.

For whatever reason,
the passion for fiercely pursuing
objects and experiences
that promise ever-lasting happiness
always overrides
the inevitable sting of suffering
that accompanies it.

Sadly, it's not until the suffering
goes deep enough
that the search for Self-knowledge
becomes a possibility
(and even then, with a little grace).

All of man's problems
are due to ignorance.

And what does it lead to?

Desire.

But perhaps more so,
fear.

Ignorance is intelligent,
and fear is its insurance

that only a handful of people
ever get to the bottom
of what's causing them to suffer.

We desire many things
to help make us feel whole,
but mostly
we fear understanding
why we feel incomplete
in the first place.

We know there's something
in our shoe,
but lack the courage
to take it out.

Tension

The intellect gains
a little knowledge
and thinks
it has it all figured out.

But the ego
won't buy it.

The tension between the two
can be insurmountable,
and old conditioning ensures
the childlike ego
won't give in.

Attachment and aversion
emerge from behind
the curtain of the subconscious
like unsolicited salesmen—
always lurking,
waiting to see
if someone will answer
the door this time.

The ego's last line of defense
is always
the threat of boredom.

But even the intellect knows
doing nothing
is not an option
for the doer/enjoyer.

As for the Self,
it's happy
to just be.

Meditation

Meditation is a conundrum.

The basic idea
is to relax
and make the mind clear—
that is,
free from obstructions
and conducive
to seeing the truth.

Although we might be able
to relax the body
by mentally scanning it
or imagining
a cleansing light,
it's almost impossible
for the mind
to relax.

At best,
the mind experiences
brief moments
of "letting go"
by focusing on the breath
or silence.

However,
the mind will only follow a task
until something
more interesting
comes along.

Then it's off
on another thought thread,
pursuing some kind
of subtle pleasure—
anything
as long as it's even slightly
more pleasurable
than the current task.

Telling the mind
what it can
and cannot do
just makes things worse.

While teachers often give
a set of instructions
for how to meditate,
this unwittingly sabotages
any chance of success.

The mind knows
what you're up to
and will refuse
to cooperate.

In the beginning,
meditation is new and exciting,
with surprising epiphanies
that keep you coming back.

But sooner or later
the mind gets bored

and decides that thinking about
what you're going to eat for dinner
is more important than viewing

the depths of being.

The best way to meditate
is to not try
to be still,
not try
to stop thoughts,
not try
to "just be,"
not try
to do anything.

Throw out
any and all agendas.

Don't even call it meditation.

As soon as you label it,

you've created an expectation
for what it should be.

But also—
don't try
to not have an agenda.

Don't try
to not label it.

Don't try
to do anything!

Can you do that?

Don't try
to answer that question.

The advice is:
don't try
to figure out meditation—
which, of course,
is what makes it
so difficult.

Meditation is supposed to be
a process of not-doing,
and yet even that
implies too much.

Meditation is like the Self.

You can only describe it
in negative terms:
"not this,"
"not that."

In the end,
meditation is as close
to the Self
as we can ever hope to get.

But don't try
to get close
to the Self.

And don't hope.

See the conundrum?

Perhaps it's just better
to seek knowledge.

At least with knowledge
you can do something—
and the mind
is happy to oblige.

A Most Peculiar Situation

Vedanta is good medicine,
but sometimes
you still get frustrated
by your own
hard-wired ignorance.

"I want enlightenment
and I want it now!"
the ego declares.

Unfortunately,
it takes time.

You're not going to erase
decades—
possibly lifetimes—
of ignorance
in six months,
six years,
or maybe ever
during your short lifespan.

Enlightenment takes time
because there's a kind of
reprogramming
that occurs.

First,
you work on getting the knowledge.

Next,
the knowledge
works on you.

It's one thing
to see the truth
and another
to have the truth
fully programmed
and assimilated.

The knowledge works on you
by chipping away
at conditioning,
slowly letting
more of the truth
come through.

Enlightenment is made difficult
by the fact that
we don't always know
what's preventing us
from obtaining it.

Maya hides the route
and won't let us see
where we're getting trapped.

This is why they say
ignorance
is intelligent.

In the end,
it's all a bewildering game.

Because it's only
the person
that wants freedom.

The Self
is already free.

The Self,
pretending to be a person
and bound,
is seeking
apparent liberation.

Why the Self
plays this game,
nobody really knows.

It's tempting to speculate
that God got bored one day
and created the world
and all its beings
to entertain itself.

But if that's the case,
God is a masochist
with no qualms
about pain
or suffering.

Before Vedanta,
I would have said
that something
wants to have an experience.

What that thing is,
and why it wants
to have an experience,
is unknown.

Why there is anything at all—
including consciousness—
just boggles the mind.

But as it turns out,
Vedanta doesn't claim
to have answers
to every question.

It would disagree with:
1.there is a thing
that wants to have an experience, and
2.there is a "why."

The Self is actionless,
attributeless,
and cannot be viewed objectively.

So it's not a thing.

Vedanta doesn't even debate
a "why."

There is no why.

Even the sages
are perplexed
by why anything exists.

There is the Self,
and there is a mysterious power
that makes the world appear.

That's it.

The fact that so few
even consider this at all
is testimony
to how distracted
we are as a society.

If everyone were qualified
for enlightenment,
we would be racing toward it together

like a steam locomotive.

Every conversation
would be about the Self—
with wonder,
amazement,
and devotion.

Instead,
we meditate on
money,
sports,
politics,
sex,
and whatever shiny object
the media puts
in front of us next.

It's like
99.9% of the population
has mental cataracts.

What a peculiar situation.

Be Happy

An unsaid rule of Vedanta
is to never trust
your feelings,
emotions
and thoughts.

Instead, one should trust
knowledge
and logic.

This is tough to practice,
as it's so ingrained in us
to constantly ask,
"How am I feeling now?"
and then act
based on whatever feeling
we are currently experiencing.

This occurs most often
when we are depressed,
fearful,
or caught
in some other negative thought.

The last thing the ego wants
to admit

is that it's being
emotional
and irrational.

The ego always wants
it its way—
logic be damned!

As humans,
we take pride
in our ability to feel
and to intuit.

We embrace feeling,
emotion,
and passion
as something
uniquely human.

It's what gives us
"soul."

The question is:

Do you want
to be right
or be happy?

Mumukshutva

Vedanta tells us that *maya*
uses its dual powers
of concealment
and projection
to put on a grand show
that fools everyone.

It's only when we put on
our non-duality glasses
that the world
comes into correct focus.

But it's hard work—
as proven by the fact
that so many of us
are fooled
most
or all
of the time.

We take the world to be real,
never questioning
the thin veneer
that separates
apparent reality
from the truth.

Perhaps it's so hard
because we can't imagine
our true essence
as a substrate
that is not objectifiable.

We can't imagine anything
outside the context
of the world.

It's like the first time
someone tells you
the universe is infinite—
it boggles the mind,
leaves you unsettled,
and maybe even disturbed
enough that you'd rather
not think about it at all.

Like an infinite universe,
we struggle to imagine
consciousness
as the ultimate substrate
of being.

We are programmed
to always look
for another support—
something behind
the last one.

"It's turtles all the way down,"
the Hindus like to say.

Most of us stop at God
as the ultimate substrate.

We're taught it's taboo
to ask questions
for which there are no answers, like

"If God created us,
who created God?"

Unable to process such ideas,
we tuck them away
in a dresser drawer
somewhere out of sight.

Vedanta isn't for wimps.

It takes guts
to want to slice open
your own flesh
and see what's inside.

Who would do such a thing?!

Answer:

Those who cannot stand

living in ignorance.

Those who sense
they are in a dreamscape
and begin to look around.

Those who want
nothing more
than to have the truth
revealed to them.

For them,
there is no holding back.

Not even the sight
of their own blood
will stop them.

They will do
their own autopsy.

They will cut deep.

They will do
whatever it takes.

They will stop at nothing
to have the truth revealed.

Vedanta has a special word

for that:

Mumukshutva—

Burning.
All-consuming.
Desire.

The Only Game in Town

One thing that becomes clear
as one actualizes Self-knowledge
is that the goal of reaching freedom
is no longer just one life objective
among many—

it's the objective.

Vedanta shows the truth.
And even though the mind
is often clouded-over,
when the teachings come into focus,
confidence in the them
becomes strong.

Sooner or later,
truth-realization becomes
the only game in town—
and everything else,
just a side show.

Even the most existential threats
become a diversion.

Nuclear war?
Global warming?

Armageddon?

…all just a spectacle
when the truth
of what we are
comes into focus.

Our ambitions die.

Fame, fortune and prestige
become non-pursuits.

A job becomes a role to play—
a means to fulfill responsibilities.

Family is a network
to help, support and instruct
when the occasion arises,
but not something
to cling to.

Life, in short,
is no longer something
to squeeze maximum pleasure from.

It's something
to be understood
to its fullest.

"Reveal all to me"

is the mantra of the wise.

The world becomes
less substantial
and more ephemeral—
more dream-like.

Not in a cartoonish way,
but through the knowledge
that everything
outside consciousness
is constantly changing
and never the same.

The wise know this world
to be like
the shifting sands of time.

It's all shifting
constantly
and continuously.

It's called *samsara*.

We ride out events,
relationships,
and the coming's and going's of life,
always anchored
in the one thing
that is unchanging,

limitless
and eternal—

the light
that makes it all possible.

Bubbles

Each of us—
celebrities,
politicians,
spiritual leaders included—
lives in a bubble.

We do our best
to make
and decorate
the bubble
to our liking.

In our bubble
is our house,
office,
city,
country,
family,
friends,
lover,
pets,
hobbies,
memories,
preferences,
objects
and beliefs.

What doesn't live
within the bubble
is the truth.

The truth
is that
which cannot be encapsulated
or shaped
to our liking.

It's what remains
even after
the bubble has burst.

The trick
is to know
you're in a bubble—
and see past it.

To have your sights
on the horizon
at all times.

And to know
that nothing can
or ever will
diminish
the truth.

The truth

is the truth.

The rest is just...

bubbles.

Dear Jiva

Dear Jiva,

You're already as good as you get. There is no further perfecting "you."

This applies to all your apparent attributes, including—but not limited to—your physical condition, psychological state, outward appearance, intelligence, virtues, spirituality, and worldly accomplishments.

This is it, bud.

Enjoy!

Love,
You

P.S.
The real you is already perfect.

Reincarnation

The whole reincarnation thing
doesn't make much sense.

The Vedas teach that after death
the mind is transferred
to a new body
and a new set of circumstances
that will facilitate our progress
toward *moksha*
—aka enlightenment.

Apparently,
we've been bouncing around
for lifetimes,
unconsciously seeking freedom.

To make it worse,
according to scripture,
it's not even the "I"
I believe I am
that bounces around.

It's just a bundle
of impersonal,
conditioned tendencies
developed over lifetimes.

Of course,
all of this sounds
like a fable—
something meant to motivate believers
toward liberation.

Nobody really knows
what happens after you die.
Logic can only take us so far.

Still,
it's fun to speculate.

Maybe death is just
changing the TV channel—
one moment you're a cowboy
in a spaghetti western,
the next moment
you're one of those blue creatures
in Avatar.

Same insecure halfwit.
Different costume.

None of this really matters
when you consider
that any memory
of a past life
would be completely erased.
What's the point

of contemplating reincarnation
if you can't remember
any of your past lives?

At that point,
it's just entertainment—
imagining post-death possibilities.

And once you know
who you are,
all of this speculation
loses its value.

Life, death, and reincarnation
become more of the same dream.

However,
based on actual worldly experience,
reincarnation might be interpreted
in a much simpler way.

We are what we inherit
from our parents.

Not just physically
—"I have my mother's eyes"—
but psychologically as well.

Personality traits,
tendencies,

talents.

At birth,
each of us inherits
a genetic ancestral map,
with the only "choice"
being which tendencies
we develop
and which we ignore.

A hereditary skill
in one century
might produce a cabinet maker.

In another,
a web developer.

We like to identify
with our interests.

But they too
are just more mom-and-dad parts,
which they inherited
from their parents,
who inherited them
from theirs—

a thread
stretching back
thousands of years.

Seen this way,
our "incarnation"
has unfolded
across generations
through countless bodies.

Reincarnation, then,
isn't mystical at all.

It's visible
in the family tree.

And once we see this,
it becomes clear
that what I am
isn't the independent "me"
I imagined.

After all,
I did nothing
to become "me."

Everything is happening
on its own momentum,
within an intricate system—
God's world.

Can you see
that there's no separation
between "you"

and your great-great-great grandfather?

If that feels uncomfortable,
can you also see
that none of it
is your fault?

"You" are just a link.

"You" are just happening—
by no will of your own.

It's all impersonal.

From this perspective,
there is no reincarnation.

There is only
continuous manifestation,
unfolding from an ancient
genetic thread.

This is the bizarre world
we live in.
This is *maya*—
where nothing is as it appears,
and ignorance
hides the truth.

Heaven

In passing conversation
about the recent death of a loved one,
someone casually says to me
they believe they will go to heaven
after they die.

I gently reply:

"Which part of you—
your body
or just your mind?"

"I don't know.
I guess some semblance
of my previous self.
 'Me' in another form?"
he says,
with a bit of agitation
for being challenged
about what is considered
a widely accepted belief.

"Okay," I ask,
"What will you do
when you get there,
and for how long

do you think heaven
will remain interesting for you?"

"How would I know..
.Jeez!"
he answers
with exasperation.

I don't press on,
but I continue to wonder
to myself
about the idea of a heaven.

Everyone pictures themselves
in an afterlife
as a younger,
better version
of their old self,
surrounded by the people
they love.

I'm not mocking it.
I'm just asking
how this would be
any different
from how things are now.

Because if it's the same
as this worldly life,
I'm afraid there

isn't much
to look forward to.

Let me explain.

If heaven were to actually exist,
it would it would still have to be
a world of opposites—
where for every up
there's a down,
and where for every gain,
some pain.

Perhaps in heaven
God programs beings differently,
so no one suffers
due to ignorance,
and everyone enjoys
their ephemeral existence
in harmony
with His laws.

Or maybe heaven
is simply having
a perfect understanding
of our experience
so that we can enjoy it
without any false expectations.
tAnyway,
heaven isn't

what people really want.

What they really want is peace—
a life free of burden.

They want a refuge
from all their agitating desires,
fears
and neurotic thoughts.

They want some respite
from the ignorance
that drives them mad
on a daily basis.

Heaven is just a concept,
one that seems probable
only because of
our dualistic perspective.

But in the end,
heaven would be
just more *samsara*.

Furthermore,
just like in this world,
in heaven,
we would eventually
begin to question
our experience

and develop a desire
to be free
from its limitations—

heavenly limitations,
but limitation, nevertheless.

What kind of limitations,
you ask?

What if I don't want
to be in heaven anymore?

What if I get bored of heaven,
get tired of it all,
and miss the grittiness
of worldly life?

If being unshackled
is our ultimate objective,
then even heaven
would be unsatisfactory.

Perhaps this is why
being alive
in this human form
is so sacred.

Because only here
can we really work

through our stuff—
 and gain the actual freedom
we ultimately seek.

Teaching Children About Death

There is something in you
that has witnessed your life
since you were born.

This something
never changes,
is never born,
and never dies.

It's a light
that illuminates the world
and your every thought.

It is the same light
that gives life
to this body
and every body.

When you die,
you lose the person—
but not the light.

That light,
which has shined forever,
even before you were born,
is pure,

infinite
and eternal.

If you're inclined to think so,
you may believe
that you will be born
in another body
to experience this world
once again.

Or, if it helps,
you can think of dying
like falling asleep.

When you're in deep sleep,
the world disappears.
The person
you believe you are
disappears.

But the real you
is still there,
happy,
at peace
just being

—just being
the light.

Bliss

All experiences
come and go.

In the end,
all that we poor souls
have to rely on
is the knowledge
that we are consciousness—
the Self.

So we learn about the Self.
We contemplate the Self.
We use it
to discriminate
between what's true
and what's not.

And we accept everything
as a blessing.

Only by the grace of God
do we become
any wiser.

One of my favorite quotes
is from Marie Curie:

Nothing in life is to be feared;
it is only to be understood.
Now is the time to understand more,
so that we may fear less.

Everyone fears.

We worry—
a lot.

It comes with the package.

I suppose the bliss
we gain
through understanding
who we are
is really about
not having to worry
anymore.

Only Then

She prefers to tell me
in a whisper,
as if it were a secret:

Most people are fine
swimming
as if it were a race to nowhere—
thrashing the water,
gazing down
into the dark,
murky depths
of the ocean.

But not me.

I prefer
to just be still,
floating on my back,
looking up
at the stars.

Only then
am I
truly happy.

Winning the Super Megalotto Jackpot

Maya is intelligent,
it fools everyone.

One of its most astonishing tricks
is that it conceals the truth.

The truth is so concealed
that nobody recognizes it—
not even the smartest among us.

We don't recognize the truth
because it is who we are.

It's like the camera
looking for itself
in the photographs.

As a result,
because we are unable
to find life's answers,
we create beliefs
and try to convince each other
of things like,
 "Jesus loves you."

When our confidence begins to falter,
we blame it on our lack of faith,
and not on the stories.

How sad.

And so we go through life,
through multiple generations,
believing that we suffer
from a lack of conviction
rather than blaming it
on the real culprit:

beautiful,
intelligent
ignorance.

My dear friend—
that you are able
to see the truth;
that you are able
to recognize it
and pick it out
from the thousands of impostors—
is nothing trivial.

Too many of us
are walking around
with a heavy boulder

strapped to our backs.

I ask:

How many of us
actually have the privilege
of unstrapping that boulder
and being free
of its tremendous
and agonizing weight?

How many of us
even recognize
that ignorance
is the very strap
that holds that boulder
to our backs?

What an amazing privilege
to see
and know
the truth.

My friend,
never forget
what you have found.

To see through the veil,
even once,
is no small grace.

And once you've seen,
you cannot unsee.

The boulder
may still be there—
but the strap
is broken.